PETER SEREFINE

Progress, Really?

One man's view of social progress in America

- A Beacon Of Common Sense -
www.Liberty-Lighthouse.com

Contents

Foreword

There is no doubt that progress can be good. It was Progress that got us out of caves and into houses. Progress gave us running water, electricity, computers, and all the comforts of modern life. There is also no question that Progress never stops. Just look at communications for example; we went from telegraphs to party line telephones to dedicated line phones. From touch tone to cordless. From cellular phones to smartphones with more computing power than all of NASA in 1969 when we put a man on the moon.

I am writing this book to look specifically at social progress. Social progress has brought a lot of good to the world. Unfortunately, social progress has also brought up even more questions for our society. I am not against progress itself, but rather blind progress: progress for the sake of progress without thought to how it will affect our country. This book is about a single question, where is social progress in America taking us?

Preface

It is important to understand where information comes from, so let me start by telling you a little about myself. I am a high school educated, middle-aged, white man, and a proud member of the middle class. I consider myself a conservative in politics, however, I have not voted for a Republican presidential candidate in the past several elections. I am not a politician or a political expert in any way. In fact, I don't consider myself an expert in any subject. In short, I am an average American man.

I have never written anything to be published before, not even a letter to the editor. I have decided to write this book partly for my own catharsis, and partly to, "Support and defend the constitution of the United States of America," much like many figures before me. The following are my observations of the changes to the American culture during my lifetime, a compilation of many of the, "signs of progress" I have witnessed. I will not attempt to tell you what to think. I only ask that you do think.

Acknowledgement

I would like to thank my primary school teachers and my parents who taught me to think for myself. I also would like to thank my fourteen-year-old son, Jack, for making me proud by showing interest while I wrote. I especially want to thank my soulmate, Staisha Hancock, for pointing out when I started ranting like a cranky old man.

1

Education

"Education is the most powerful weapon which you can use to change the world"
~ Nelson Mandela ~

* * *

School - education outside of the home - is where it all begins. When I started going to school in the late 1970s, every school day started with the Pledge of Allegiance and a silent prayer. Soon an argument was made about the separation of church and state. It was deemed inappropriate to hold a mandatory silent prayer in a public school. So while I was still in elementary school, the silent prayer was renamed, "a moment of silence." It was explained to us that not everyone prayed, so to be more inclusive a moment of silence would now be observed. This would allow those that wished to pray to do so, but we could also meditate or think about whatever we wanted, as long as we were silent. That seems reasonable, right? As I will try to illustrate in the course of this book, Progress is never satisfied. It didn't take long for the moment of silence to be eliminated by many school districts.

Next came the attack on the Pledge of Allegiance itself, simply because it contains the word "God". In 2000, Elk Grove United School District in California argued in court that even listening to, "under God" violated students' first amendment rights. On February 19, 2019, ABC News reported that students in Connecticut were now being allowed to skip the Pledge of Allegiance. That isn't enough, says progress. I've heard news stories recently that tell of children being chastised because they prayed over their lunch in a school cafeteria or had the audacity to read a bible during downtime in the school day. I am not a religious man, but how is a child praying over their lunch harmful or disruptive to the other students?

Across our nation, Christmas is being removed from public school too. Christmas trees are called "holiday" trees if allowed at all. Christmas break is now Winter recess. Easter is not even mentioned, even though it was the reason Spring break was created and often falls within the Spring break. Either the progressive mantra of inclusivity or the demand for separate church and state seems to mandate the removal of Christianity from the education system. The separation of church and state seems to be just a guise for advancing Progress. The constitution forbids a state-sanctioned religion, but God is referenced all through our country's history. There is not one single mention of a specific faith. Isn't that the key to separate church and state?

Entirely removing God from school was just the beginning of progress. Next comes the physical reminders of our nation's history – the works of art that adorn the parks and public spaces all across our nation. Statues of Confederate soldiers and generals are being removed because of their connection to our history of slavery. Suddenly, the mere presence of a monument that has stood undisturbed for decades is so offensive to Progress that it must be torn down. What these Confederates may have done before or after the Civil War seems to be irrelevant. For example, the Confederate general "Stonewall" Jackson taught slaves to read and write before the war, even though it was against the law in Virginia to do so. Progress has looked back 150 years, through the lens of modern morality, and judged that representation of history equals glorification; anything and anyone that was not on the side of abolition is unworthy of a page in our history. The sentence for their judgment is the destruction of works of art. Shouldn't a nation teach both the good and bad parts of its own history?

Speaking of history, now our National holidays are under attack. Society is turning Christopher Columbus into a demon. The movement to rename Columbus Day to Indigenous People's day is gaining strength. Notre Dame University recently covered over murals of Columbus. These murals were painted in the 1880s. For almost 140 years these impressive paintings adorned the hall to inspire students. Now they are offensive. I don't know how much Columbus was personally responsible for the massacres of the native peoples - maybe he was a brutal murderer - but the fact remains, without his courage and his astonishing conviction, our country would not exist. Sure, someone would have eventually crossed the Atlantic Ocean and returned to Europe, but what are the chances that the Land of the Free and the Home of the Brave would have come into existence at a time in history when a group of colonists could have defeated the all-powerful British empire?

The progress in education is certainly not restricted to primary school either. The fact that colleges and universities across our country lean heavily progressive is well documented. I have seen several studies that identify the ratio of progressive professors to conservative professors somewhere between ten and thirteen to one. In a Washington Times article dated October 6th, 2016, it is estimated at twelve to one. The ratio of progressive to conservative commencement speakers is almost identical at about ten to one. These mostly progressive professors are teaching students – and those students will increasingly earn an utterly useless degree. I used to laugh at Art History degrees. I always wondered what job anyone who earned one of these degrees could do that put their degree to work, except maybe teach. There are now a plethora of degrees that beg the same question. Shouldn't the goal of a college education be valuable long-term employment?

When I was finishing high school, I was not sure what career path I wanted to take. I already had four years of restaurant experience and I did not want to spend tens of thousands of dollars on a degree that I was not sure that I would use. I knew I wanted to serve in the military, so I didn't even apply to any colleges. After my enlistment, I went back to the restaurant industry, but as a manager now. I had been working in restaurants for several years when I decided to make the hospitality industry my career of choice. I was in my early twenties and already in management. By then, the cost of a hospitality degree just didn't seem worth it.

School is supposed to be the place where we learn what is printed in the textbooks and where we learn to interact with other people, some of whom have different beliefs than we do. School is where we learn how to be social. Well, the school *used* to be where we learned to be social. Over sixty percent of colleges now have speech codes restricting what students can say on campus. Administrators regularly deny speakers the opportunity to speak on campus because they don't agree with the speaker's point of view, even after a student group invites the speaker. Today, a college student must go out of their way to find a point of view that is not progressive. Is it a well-rounded education if it is so obviously one-sided?

We have all heard the phrase, "history is written by the victor," and right now, Progress appears to be the victor. Another phrase that Progress seems to be ignoring is, "history repeats itself." I have often said if Napoleon had learned the lesson of the Russian winter from Caesar then the entire world would speak French, and if Hitler had learned that same lesson from Napoleon then we would all be speaking German. So, look at the history of the world. Who else rewrote their own national history and tore down statues? Isn't this consistently one of the first steps of socialist, communist, and fascist revolutions throughout world history?

2

Everyone is Special

"Always remember that you are absolutely unique. Just like everyone else."
~ Margaret Mead ~

* * *

My children are special – to me. Every parent feels that way. Every person is special in some way. I firmly believe that. Progress seems to view this a little differently.

I think this part of progress started a little before my time. I am fond of blaming Dr. Spock. No, not Spock from Star Trek. Dr. Benjamin Spock, MD. Dr. Spock was a pediatrician who wrote the book *Baby and Child Care* in 1946. He was the first to really publish anything on pediatric psychoanalysis for the public. Psychoanalysis itself is a set of theories and therapy for treating mental illness and is sometimes referred to as pseudo-science. Dr. Spock took these already questionable theories and applied them to raising children. He successfully advocated "time out" as punishment or negative reinforcement for children. Again, that seems like a reasonable suggestion, but Progress rarely stops with a reasonable suggestion.

Before I get into corporal punishment, I would like to state that I am not making an argument for or against it. I only wish to point out how progress is removing it as an option for parents. I can recall getting spanked only a few times as a child, but I remember deserving them. Well, except one. I swear to this day, I didn't do that one thing that I got spanked for, but I digress. When I was in elementary school, corporal punishment was allowed if the parents gave the school permission. The next step in the march of Progress was to eliminate corporal punishment from the school system. Again, arguably a reasonable progression. The march goes on. Many states decided that controlling the discipline inside of the school system wasn't enough. Those states made laws forbidding corporal punishment entirely. Parents found to violate these laws could be charged with child abuse. On a side note, I knew at least one kid who took advantage of these laws by calling child protective services and falsely accusing his step-father because the child didn't get something he wanted. By no means am I advocating for child abuse, I want to make that perfectly clear. I am simply pointing out how Progress has expanded the definition of child abuse. Short of abuse, shouldn't decisions about discipline be made by parents?

Let's get back to school. Grades are important within any school system. I went to school in several different districts in three different states. My first memory of the grading scale was A, B, C, D, and F. These letter grades equated to Excellent, Above Average, Average, Below Average, and Fail, respectively.

There was also an I, for incomplete. The first effect of Progress I remember regarding grades was that the F, which meant Fail, was changed to E. Thanks to Dr. Spock's book and other published works on pediatric psychoanalysis, we now know that failure can be painful. Progress determined that the stigma of the word fail could be damaging to a student's ego. Progress is like the drill sergeant calling cadence, left, right, left. Keep marching on.

Now let us look at the meaning of those letter grades more closely. The letter grade C means average. By definition, most students should get a C, most of the time. However, the average isn't special. Average doesn't make the student feel good. Average doesn't get a child accepted to college. That brings us to what is going on regarding school grades now, twenty-eight years after my high school graduation. A recent news story covered several districts that have instituted minimum grades. That is a minimum score of 50% recorded for all school work. So, a student who doesn't even complete an assignment or doesn't even show up for an exam is given a 50% grade instead of their actual grade or an incomplete. Progress has chosen to give a minimum grade rather than run the risk of hurting a students' feelings. Dr. Spock's psychoanalysis is being used to protect the emotions of the student at the expense of a true grade. This story made national news on September 25, 2018, when Newsweek reported that one eighth-grade teacher in Florida was fired because she opposed the policy and refused to give a 50% score to a student who earned a zero. What is the true value of a grade if half of it is given away freely to some? How can Progress assess true excellence or hard work if there is no failure? Without failure when young, how do students grow the strength to overcome failure in their adult lives? In short, how is this policy fair to the students who finish all of the work?

Protecting feelings and emotions seems to be a huge issue for the progress of society. Colleges and Universities have designated "free speech zones" as defined areas where potentially hurtful speech is permitted. Let that sink in for a moment. Colleges that are largely subsidized by your tax dollars and charge increasingly exorbitant tuitions are restricting the first amendment rights of our students to a designated area. These same institutions of higher learning have created "safe places" for when the students' feelings do get hurt. Every student is so special that one student is forbidden to say anything, do anything, or wear anything, that could possibly offend another person. What are these policies teaching the students?

Now that we are on the topic of Colleges and Universities, who should go to college? Progress seems to have decided that everyone should go to college, not that everyone should have the *chance* to go to college. Our society seems to have forgotten about the other post-primary school options. I chose to enlist in the US Navy, a decision that I have never regretted. Trade and vocational schools look like great options for the average person, but there are no more average people in a progressive society. Since everyone is special, then everyone should be smart enough, organized enough, and ambitious enough to earn a college degree. I have said many times, soon it will cost more to hire a plumber or electrician than a lawyer or doctor. It's simple supply and demand. If everyone goes to college, what will that college degree really be worth? If everyone is special, then what does special really mean? Is Progress trying to change the meaning of the word special?

That brings up the cost of college. Progress suggests that

every child is special, then nearly demands that every child goes to college. Obviously, not everyone can afford college, so many people end up with tens of thousands of dollars in debt after attending college, even if they don't graduate and earn a degree. That is where Progress steps in again. Progress wants you and I, taxpayers, to forgive these student debts. After all, if everyone is so special, then why should they have to pay for an education? Oh, and don't forget, most of these people will end up in a career that has nothing to do with the degree they may have earned. People are staying home and living with their parents well into their twenties, often because they can't get employed in their industry of choice. Thirty-three percent of people between the ages of 25 and 29 live with their parents according to census.gov in August 2017. That is the highest percentage of stay-at-home adult children in 75 years. So, neither the taxpayers nor many students seem to get many benefits from the degrees. Regardless of who pays, does anyone benefit?

Another way Progress has made everyone special is the concept that everyone gets a trophy. When I was young, I remember getting a certificate of participation at the beginning of a science fair. You had to earn one of the top three grades to receive a ribbon or a trophy. Those ribbons and trophies meant a lot after all the hard work you put into earning it. If you wanted a trophy and didn't earn it this time, you tried harder next time. The emotional pain of a special child walking away from a competitive event without a trophy was just too much for progress. Now, many events give a trophy for participation. If everyone gets a trophy, then what is the point of working to get better? What does a child learn from a participation trophy, other than that they are special – just like everyone else?

3

Entitlement

"Successful people have a sense of gratitude. Unsuccessful people have a sense of entitlement."
~ Steven Aitchison ~

* * *

The next natural step after making everyone special is that everyone feels entitled. After all, if you are so special shouldn't you always get whatever you want? We parents have created children that feel entitled to whatever they want. We give them expensive video gaming systems that use expensive games and subscriptions. We give them smartphones and pay for their service. We hover over them as they are involved in every activity and sport that they show even the slightest interest in. We buy their cars and pay the insurance. Is there any wonder so many more kids are living at home well into their twenties and beyond?

I don't think I ever felt entitled. Sure, my parents gave me an allowance, but I wanted more. I was mowing lawns for money as soon as I was big enough to push the mower that I bought at a yard sale. When I was fourteen, I got a work permit and a summer job at Savard's Family Restaurant in Watkins Glen, New York. The next summer, when I was fifteen, I went back to that same place for a summer job again. By the time I was sixteen, I was working year-round. I have been employed and paying taxes ever since. I started at minimum wage and worked my way up. After that first summer or maybe the second summer, I don't think that I was ever paid minimum wage again. There is a big push now to make the minimum wage a *living wage*. Progress seems to think that every job should pay well enough to support a family. Why does a part-time after-school job need to pay enough to support a family?

The federal minimum wage was $3.35 per hour when I got my first tax-paying job, in 1987. Adjusting for inflation, that would be $7.45 today. The current federal minimum wage is $7.25. It looks like the minimum wage has kept up with inflation pretty well, but Progress disagrees. Progress has already convinced fourteen states to raise the minimum wage to $10 per hour or more. Five other states have also passed legislation to raise the minimum wage over $10 per hour in the next few years. Many of these now nineteen states plan to raise the minimum wage to $15 or more. That is more than double the current federal minimum wage. What will this do to the cost of goods and services in these states? How much more buying power will someone earning minimum wage really have after prices adjust? Simply put, how much will you and I have to pay for a visit to the local fast food place if the wages of the employees double?

This sense of entitlement does not stop at childhood. Progress appears to want the government to take care of all of us from cradle to grave. 21% of people and 49% of households in America accepted some sort of need-based entitlement benefit in 2012. Over the past forty-five years, federal spending on entitlement programs has increased by 1060%. In that same forty-five years, the Gross Domestic Product (GDP) has only increased by 270%. According to demographic information on recipients, race and political views don't matter much. White, Black, Hispanic, Democrat, Republican, or Independent portions of the population all receive benefits at similar rates. The one demographic that I find shocking is that 39% of people earning over $100,000 a year receive some sort of entitlement benefit. It seems that asking for government assistance is no longer a last resort. Progress has made applying for government assistance the first thought of many people. Progress still isn't satisfied. Progress is always trying to add new entitlements. This is very expensive to us, the taxpaying citizens. I specify *tax paying* citizens because about 45% of citizens don't pay any federal income tax, according to a Market Watch article on February 26th, 2019. What would this bit of "progress" look like if we were to put it into a feasibility model?

Many of these entitlement programs are part of the war on poverty. President Johnson declared the war on poverty in 1964. Now there are seventy different means-tested federal entitlement programs. None of these programs do anything to help or even encourage the recipients to rise above their dependence on government aid. Since L.B.J. declared the war on poverty over $16 trillion, or over $47,000 per person in America, has been spent in its name. That is over 70% of the current national debt. UC Davis reports that the poverty rate in 1964 was 19% of the population and in 2017 it was 12.3%. All of those tax dollars have not even lowered the poverty rate in America by 7%. Is this really effective use of our tax dollars? Is this actually doing anything to end poverty? Rather than entitlements wouldn't gainful employment be more valuable to the poor, more helpful to society, and more fiscally responsible to the taxpayer?

4

Sexuality

"Sexuality is the great field of battle between biology and society."
~ Nancy Friday ~

* * *

Over the course of my life, I have seen sexuality become a big issue in our society. Like most people my age, I grew up with the understanding that there are two genders. male and female, and that everyone was either heterosexual or homosexual. Progress no longer considered homosexuality to be a mental illness and insisted that being homosexual was not a choice. People were born either straight or gay. This once simple concept of a male and a female of our species has now become convoluted and confusing. Heterosexual and homosexual have been expanded into every color of the rainbow – and then some.

I had also heard of strange and rare cases of transgender

people. It was my understanding that being transgender was the extremely rare instance of a male brain trapped in a female's body or vice versa. Sooner or later the LGB community (Lesbian - Gay -Bisexual) embraced transgender people and added the letter T to their acronym. The LGBT community stayed that way for quite some time. By 2015 states were passing laws regarding public restrooms. At least one of these laws stated that a person must use the restroom that correlated to the gender printed on their birth certificate. This law was apparently so discriminatory to the transgender community that in 2016 President Barack Obama proclaimed, by executive order, that a person could use the restroom of their chosen gender identity. That executive order threatened to withhold federal education funding from the individual states if they did not comply. Citizens that identified as transgender in 2016 were less than 1% of the population, 0.6% by most reports. By Presidential decree, transgenderism had instantly become mainstream.

That was about three years ago, and since Progress is never satisfied, society is now telling us there are 63 genders. In fact, aPATH.org published a big chart to explain the 63 genders in 2000. Now there are masculine, feminine, heterosexual, homosexual, and bisexual versions of males, females, andradites, and hermaphrodites. Progress has apparently decided that any sexual preference equates to a gender. The former LGB community, not willing to be outdone by society at large is now known as the LGBTQIAA community. I don't even know what all those additional letters stand for. It is all just Orwellian newspeak to me. I understand that there are vast and diverse preferences in the world. Does that mean that there are also vast and diverse genders?

Having established the idea of 63 genders was not enough for our progressive society either. Now gender is being presented as a choice. This really confuses me. Progress denied for generations that homosexuality was a choice, but suddenly gender is? This idea made news when new parents refused to allow the gender to be "assigned" on certificates of birth. NBC News told us about how these new parents intend to keep their children in a complete state of gender neutrality until such time the children can discover for themselves on July 19th, 2018. The state of New York now has a third option for gender on birth certificates. In addition to M for males and F for females X can now be printed on birth certificates to identify gender-neutral.

New parents aren't the only agents of progress to subscribe to the concept of gender as a choice. Colleges and universities have adopted this idea too. The University of Michigan established that students were to choose by which pronoun they were to be called, and the faculty were instructed to honor the students' choice. This story made the Washington Post on October 7th, 2016 when that college objected to one student's choice of "your majesty" as their pronoun.

Indoctrination to this progressive sexuality begins at very young ages now and is being facilitated by our own government. Drag Queen Story Hour is an initiative moving quickly across public libraries. This movement has become popular enough that the American Library Association made resources available for when there is push back. This initiative is just what it sounds like. Men dressed as women read to children in public libraries. At least one of these drag queens, in Houston, was a convicted child sex offender. He had been charged with sexual assault of a 14-year-old in 2008. The Houston Public Library admitted that the volunteer never completed the background check and apologized. How was this allowed to happen? Did any of the parents know that beforehand?

Public schools are helping with this indoctrination too. At an elementary school in Arlington, Virginia, a transgender advocate was permitted to read a book to at least one kindergarten class. The book, I am Jazz, is a children's story about a transgender child. After reading the book, the advocate said that she was like Jazz. When she was born her parents, doctors, and all adults thought she was a boy, but she always knew she was a girl. After some of the parents complained about the event the school admitted that they did not give parents the opportunity to opt-out of the planned event. Was this just a simple oversight, or is parental permission not required for the progressive movement?

You may say, you're a straight man. Why do you care? Let's look at a few great American institutions for the effects of this progress in sexuality. The Boy Scouts of America have existed for over a hundred years. They are a privately-run non-profit organization. In their hundred-year history, they served one simple purpose, to make men out of boys; strong, independent, functional men. It is safe to say that they served that purpose well. Every man that walked on the moon earned the highest rank in the Boy Scouts, Eagle Scout. Four US presidents have been involved with scouting. This is quite an accomplishment considering there have only been eleven presidents that could have been Boy Scouts. President Gerald Ford achieved the rank of Eagle Scout. Apparently, that wasn't good enough for our progressive society.

My earliest recollection of controversy regarding sexuality and the Boy Scouts was about the time when I was transitioning from Cub Scout to Boy Scout. That would have been in the early 1980s. At that time the idea of allowing openly homosexual scouts and/or scoutmasters was in the news. Now, roughly thirty years later, the Boy Scouts of America allows girls, boys, heterosexual, homosexual, transgender, and any other proposed gender to be a scout. In fact, they have dropped "Boy" from their name entirely. On February 3rd, 2019 in Tennessee, the first all-girl "scout troop" was sworn in, according to DNJ.com. Just a few days shy of the Boy Scouts 109th-anniversary Progress celebrated this as a big win. The news also recently covered a story suggesting that condoms be provided at camp since it was no longer a male-only excursion. How can this privately-run non-profit organization stay true to its original purpose? The Boy Scouts no longer exist as they once did. Instead of creating their own organization for the acceptance of people from all gender and sexual backgrounds, Progress took the Boy Scouts and made it something else. If the large, great, and fruitful Boy Scouts of America can be forced by public pressure and many lawsuits to abandon the very principles that it was founded on, then what could be next? Only time will tell what this change has already done to the value of working very hard to earn that honorable rank of Eagle Scout.

The boy scouts are not the only organization affected by this progression in sexuality. High school sports have been shaken hard too. Locker rooms are uncomfortable enough when half of the people in them are going through puberty and the other half haven't started yet. Add a new layer of confusion by introducing an individual – who is biologically the opposite sex but identifies as your gender – into the room. Then add a biological boy into a girl's sporting event, because he identifies as a girl. In the state of Texas, for example, a boy that identifies as a girl has won the girls state championship in wrestling two years in a row, according to NBC News on February 25th, 2018. In Connecticut, an Associated Press article from February 24th, 2019 tells us of two biological boys that both identify as girls that won first and second place in a track championship. Of course, Progress is not willing to stop with high school sports either. The International Olympic Committee has begun looking into rules to allow transgender people to compete as the gender of their choice. Is any of this fair to anyone involved?

Another great American institution is currently in the news struggling with progressive sexuality. The US Military was exclusively a straight person's club until 1994 when the Don't Ask Don't Tell policy was enacted by President Bill Clinton. Before I continue, let me make one thing clear: when I was a sailor, I would not have cared if the man next to me identified himself as a female pansexual anteater, as long as he did his job and had my back. That does not mean sexuality doesn't create questions and potential problems for the military. In 2011, Don't Ask Don't Tell was repealed, allowing gay people to serve openly. Now the struggle for progress's sexuality issues pertaining to the military is happening in courts. Should transgender individuals be allowed to serve? If they are permitted to serve, which gender's uniform do they wear? Which barrack do they reside in? Which physical standard are they held to? Should the military, and ultimately the taxpayers, pay for their hormone therapy or gender reassignment surgery?

The US military has never claimed to be an equal opportunity employer. There is a very long list of things that can disqualify an individual from serving in our armed forces. You cannot enlist if you are too tall, too short, too fat, too skinny, have flat feet, a criminal history, are an addict, or many other reasons.

So why has the question of if a transgender individual should be allowed to serve become such a big deal in the media and in the court system? Could it be exclusively for the purpose of advancing the narrative of progress? Is it sensationalism?

5

Morality

* * *

This is the chapter that caused such a stir within me that I felt compelled to write this book. This chapter is largely on one of the most divisive topics in America: abortion. However, don't worry, I am not going to make a pro-life or pro-choice stance. I am not going to debate Roe v. Wade. I am not interested in the same arguments that we have all heard for either stance. All that I really want to discuss here is the recent late-term abortion legislation.

As far as I am concerned, the Supreme Court has adjudicated that abortion is legal. Period. Regardless of personal opinion regarding the morality of abortion as a whole, a vast majority of people agree that at some point during pregnancy a fetus becomes a baby, a separate individual human life. When that change happens can be debated ad nauseam. As far as I know, every state has, or at least had, drawn a line somewhere in the prenatal timeline at which point abortion was no longer an option. I say, at least had, because of the recent legislation adopted by my home state of New York.

Maybe adopted wasn't the right word. Celebrated is more accurate. Until this new legislation, New York had drawn the deadline for abortion at the 24-week mark. The new law that was celebrated by the lawmakers – and that was cast upon the freedom tower in the pink glow of reproductive rights – removed this mark. This law did not just move the line, it removed it entirely. That means a woman who is nine months pregnant, dilating, and having contractions can have an abortion if she can get the consent of a doctor. At that point, the baby is fully developed and can obviously feel pain. By that time, couldn't the baby be delivered, either naturally or via C-section, and adopted by someone who desperately wants a baby? Please, please think about that.

One unintended consequence, at least I hope it was not intended, showed itself less than a month later. A man surrendered to police after allegedly stabbing his pregnant girlfriend to death. His girlfriend was five months pregnant. He allegedly focused his stabbing at his girlfriend's belly. Shortly after his arrest, the district attorney announced that the man would not be charged with a double murder, as is usual and customary. The new law in New York had removed the killing of an unborn child from the criminal code. Killing an unborn child is now some sort of administrative or process infraction. The District Attorney could only charge him with one instance of second-degree murder, and nothing else.

Can Progress possibly push this already divisive topic further? Of course, it can. Almost immediately after New York lawmakers applauded their new law, Virginia introduced similar legislation. The governor of Virginia was the instrument of progress this time. The governor – a pediatrician, it is important to note – advocated that even after a baby is delivered that termination might still be an option. I simply cannot understand how that is not murder. How can that stance possibly correspond to the first rule of the Hippocratic oath, "do no harm"?

You might think that two states aren't really a marker for progress. Even if that is true, worry not, my friends, several other states have already introduced legislation similar to New York and Virginia. Only time will tell if Progress is successful in advancing these bills into laws. The US Senate, in an effort to slow down progress in this area, introduced a bill. The bill they were trying to pass protected children that were born alive, specifically after a failed abortion. The bill referred to as the "Born-Alive Abortion Survivors Protection Act", guaranteed medical treatment once the child was born alive. Progress blocked the bill on February 25th, 2019. Progressive senators that voted against the bill view this as a victory for abortion rights, even though the bill only protected babies that had already been born. Is this infanticide or just the first step toward eugenics?

The normalization of late-term abortion is only one of the outward signs of our progressive morality. I think the mass shooting phenomenon is a second sign. Mass shootings could also have been influenced by the same points made in the earlier chapter: everyone is special. It is more likely a combination of the progress pertaining to morality coupled with the agony children feel when reality shows them that they aren't that special. Progress itself can't accept any part of the blame, so instead society blames the gun. Guns have been prolific in the United States since before we were the United States. There was a time, even during my life, when every pickup truck at every rural high school in this country had at least one rifle hanging inside it. Has the gun changed so drastically during the past 200 years to cause mass shootings? The technology or mechanics of firearms has not changed much since World War I. The same handgun designed for use by the US Military in 1911 is not only still available, but it is also still very popular. Fully automatic weapons have been banned for decades and semi-automatic weapons have been around for over 100 years. So honestly ask yourself, what has changed? Maybe, just maybe, the progress of society has created this phenomenon. Has putting so much focus on feelings and emotions instead of results and accomplishments made people incapable of managing the disappointments of everyday life? Has our collective morality progressed to a point where this is acceptable behavior to many people?

Another indicator of serious social unrest is the suicide rate. This number has been used as a bellwether since the turn of the twentieth century. In every developed western nation, the suicide rate has declined since 1999, except in the United States. In our great nation, the suicide rate has risen 33% since 1999, according to the CDC. Before Progress tries to blame the availability of handguns, I would like to also point out methods of suicide are also tracked. In that same time period, 1999-2017, the use of handguns and poison for suicide has declined. Has our country become so terrible that more and more people feel that they have no way out, or has suicide become less taboo?

that they have no way out, or has suicide become less taboo?

6

Political Correctness

* * *

Which of these is the politically correct term; handicapped,
disabled, crippled, or differently-abled? I grew up knowing
the word handicapped was the most widely used. In the late
1990's I got to attend a class for an employer that was all about
inclusion and "ouch words." Those words are now referred
to as "trigger words". In this class, I learned the origin of the
term handicapped. In case you don't know, it dates back to
beggars having their caps in their hands begging for change. I
can see now how that could possibly offend some people. The
politically correct term of disabled was adopted by Progress
and became widely used. That is better, right? It isn't better

enough, apparently. There has been a recent push to start using the phrase differently-abled. Masking the issue doesn't make it less prevalent, it just makes us less likely to face it. Why are we trying to soften the truth?

The progress from the phrase handicapped is one simple, easily illustrated example of political correctness. There are countless more. One of the most current examples I have already touched on is transgenderism. Progress expects you and I to use the pronoun that correlates to a person's chosen gender, but with 63 genders how can we know what that is? Assuming someone's gender has become offensive. So, a doctor could cause offense while giving a prostate exam, simply by saying "sir". I guess the doctor will need to invest in political correctness insurance in addition to malpractice coverage.

Progress has made hurting feelings or offending others akin to a high crime. Progress is putting one person's feelings ahead of another person's right of free speech and in some cases ahead of religious freedom too. This is not just limited to the words that we use either. The beloved children's movie character Mary Poppins is under attack as being racist because of a scene where she is covered in soot. USA Today reported on February 4th, 2019 that Mary Poppins is dancing on rooftops with chimney sweeps in the "offensive" scene. Progress has said that a white woman with soot on her face is the same as if she had performed in blackface. USA Today also reported on November 29th, 2018 the accusation that the iconic Dr. Seuss was racist. Progress said his fantastic fictional characters all had stereotypical qualities resembling people of color – or was it because he separated red fish and blue fish? Maybe it was because he didn't like green eggs and ham?

The NFL (National Football League) has had serious PC

issues. When the players started protesting on the field by kneeling during the national anthem, I believe it was political correctness that kept the league from reacting. The coaches, managers, and owners were afraid to do anything to stop the protesters lest they be called racist. What I can't understand is that the players are employees. Employees are generally not allowed to protest while working, at least not without the consent of the company they work for. Yes, the players have an absolute right to protest, protected by the first amendment, but not necessarily while "on the clock". Team owners were paralyzed by the fear of being perceived as politically incorrect.

Major League Baseball (MLB) has just made an announcement too. ESPN said on February 7th, 2019 that political correctness has caused professional baseball to drop the term disabled list. After being the officially used term since the 1960s, players unable to play for medical reasons will now be placed on an injured list. The disabled list was unofficially used for nearly 100 years, and officially used for about fifty years. Now, suddenly beginning with the 2019 season, it is no longer acceptable. Isn't being unable to perform the duties of a job due to illness or injury the definition of disabled? What is the point of all this wordplay? Does it really change anything in our physical reality?

People can be offended by the hat that you wear, the flag you fly, the political party you join, if you eat meat, the vehicle that you drive, or if you have more money than they do. Progress has created the micro-aggression, a term coined by a psychiatrist and Harvard University professor in 1970 to describe insults and dismissals whether intentional or not. Then Progress made almost everything that we do or say into a micro-aggression. It seems like the only way to avoid offending each other would be if we all were in the same political party, all wore the same clothes, all had the same haircuts, and all had the same amount of money. Does that sound like liberty or the pursuit of happiness?

"I am offended" has become a shield that is supposed to instantly end a discussion. I was taught that "sticks and stones will break my bones, but words will never hurt me". Obviously, words can hurt, but I think what that little saying was trying to teach children is that everyone has their own opinion and someone else's opinion shouldn't hurt you. People should have enough control over their own emotions to not allow another person's opinion to hurt their feelings. Does Progress really want to control We The People to the point of censorship for the sake of hurt feelings?

Progress has now enlisted governments to try to remove any possible microaggression. Several municipalities are eliminating "man" as a prefix or suffix, turning a manhole into a utility hole. Daily Mail, in April 2011, reported that a Seattle school district has renamed Easter eggs to spring spheres. Even if you don't want to use the term Easter, eggs are not spheres. Several school districts across the country have renamed Christmas trees to holiday trees. One especially notable change was when Santa Claus was forbidden from saying his iconic catchphrase, "Ho ho ho," because it could offend women. At what point has a PC culture gone too far?

Political correctness is not universal in a progressive society. There seem to be special classes of people that are protected by political correctness while others are not. One example reported by Fox News on March 12th, 2019 when an Ohio high school student was suspended. The student arrived at school one day to find that the GSA (Gay-Straight Alliance) club had posted the rainbow gay pride flags throughout her school. The student responded by posting bible verses in the hallways of the school. The next day she received an in-school suspension for abuse, disrespect, and rudeness toward others. Aren't the acts of posting bible verses and the posting of rainbow flags equally politically charged? Aren't they both free speech?

7

Labor Unions

"Labor disgraces no man; unfortunately, you occasionally find men who disgrace labor."
~ Ulysses S. Grant ~

* * *

Labor unions are another group that illustrates progress. There is no doubt that unions were formed for very good reasons. Organizing first employees and later entire trades allowed workers to begin to be treated fairly by the wealthy business owners. This organization allowed workers leverage that they never had before as individuals. Unions, with this new leverage, brought about the forty-hour five-day workweek, employer health insurance, sick pay, paid vacations, and more. This arguably created a true middle class in our society.

I have been both a member of unions and a member of management. I have witnessed benefits from both sides of the table as well. Collective bargaining, for example, can be beneficial to both sides of the agreement. It requires negotiation to keep two groups of people happy. Having observed both sides with a few different unions causes me to pause. It seems that the good that came from unionizing wasn't enough for Progress.

Unions have grown from groups of employees gathered for protecting members' rights and for fair pay and benefits, into giant organizations that seem more concerned with their own power than the members they represent. Unions have become wealthy and powerful political organizations. Corruption has found its way into many labor unions, as often happens with many large, wealthy, and powerful organizations. According to the National Legal and Policy Center in 2015 alone, a former president of the Jacksonville Fraternal Order of Police pled guilty to helping himself to $570,000. Three union officials in New York City were charged with illegal kickbacks and stealing $1,000,000 from union health plans. Those are just two of the top ten labor union corruption stories of the year.

Collective bargaining agreements or union contracts have become bloated and confusing. These documents take simple concepts and add so many stipulations that you almost need an attorney to sort them out. There was a time when a union was so proud of its products that the union would even help management eliminate unproductive employees. I have personally seen unions fight very hard for employees that even the other employees and union members didn't think worthy of the fight. How does fighting for an unworthy employee help the rest of the members of that union? Why has it become an "us versus them" scenario?

One purpose of these agreements and contracts is to protect employees and the work hours available to those employees.

Specifying which employees can perform which duties is one common way of protecting members. These rules sound good. They certainly are made for a noble purpose; however, these rules also destroy teamwork at the worksite. One employee is forbidden from helping another for fear of the dreaded grievance. I can remember having to call maintenance to light an oven's pilot light while I was working as a cook. I was perfectly capable of lighting the pilot light in under a minute, but instead of crossing trade union lines, I had to call down and wait for a member of maintenance to arrive to do the less than a one-minute job. Isn't teamwork valuable too?

Speaking of the grievance, that process was designed to give an employee the opportunity to report an instance of unfair treatment. It is an official means of negotiating, if necessary, to solve an issue. Unfortunately, Progress has turned this valuable tool into a petty slight. The overuse of the grievance as a means of simple resistance to change, or just to be a thorn in the side of management has made them almost laughable. I recently saw a grievance threatened in my own workplace because an employee thought, incorrectly, that they would have to walk four more steps during their eight-hour workday. Management moved a piece of equipment about four steps further away from the employee's workstation. What the employee didn't realize is that the new location consolidated two stops that the employee had to make once a day. The new setup was a more efficient use of both time and space to everyone involved. The threat of the grievance seemed to be just resistance to change or possibly just a slight directed at management. How is that for efficient use of your union dues?

8

Government

"Politicians and diapers must be changed often, and for the same reason."
~ Mark Twain ~

* * *

Which came first, progressive society or big government? I don't know the answer to that question, but the two are intertwined. You could even say that they are two sides of the same coin. I have already touched on some of the ways that a progressive government has been involved in each of the preceding chapters, now I am going to look specifically at governmental progress.

The number of people our country has in jails and prisons is reaching epidemic proportions. The United States has the highest incarceration rate in the entire world. The percentage of Americans in jail or prison has risen by 700% since 1970. Is this because Progress has created so many new laws? Could this be because of progressive morality? Maybe it is a little of both. At an average annual cost of over $30,000 per inmate and about 2.2 million inmates, it sure is getting expensive. That is an average annual bill to the taxpayers of over $66 billion.

I have already covered the progress in the arena of morality, so what about the progress around laws? It seems that every time anything bad happens Progress rushes to create a new law. The obvious example of this is the rush to pass more gun control laws every time there is a mass shooting. Thousands of new laws take effect on January 1st every year, in cities and states all over the country. Cats, dogs, and rabbits can no longer be sold in California pet stores unless they come from animal shelters. Cyberbullying was made a misdemeanor in Michigan. New York now requires sexual harassment training for all employees. Cities and states all over the country have banned single-use plastic straws and stirrers. Massachusetts and New Jersey now require all residents to have health insurance. New York City once banned soft drinks over thirty-two ounces. With Progress creating literally thousands of new laws every year, who can keep up?

All these new laws remind me of one of my favorite quotes. Benjamin Franklin said, "Those who would give up essential Liberty, to purchase a little temporary Safety, deserve neither Liberty nor Safety." With so many new laws, someone is bound to break them. What do we do with offenders? Here in the US, it seems we just lock them up. In fact, we have almost 1% of our population incarcerated. Of the 2.2 million people we have locked up, about 25% are there for lower-level non-violent crimes. That is about 550,000 people. At over $30,000 per year each, that's well over $16 billion a year to keep low-level nonviolent offenders incarcerated. Why has Progress decided it necessary to imprison them with such a high cost to us, the taxpayers? Wouldn't fines and community service be more helpful to society?

Throughout modern history, some of the most tyrannical dictators started their rise to power as socially progressive. Vladimir Lenin was a progressive turned socialist who was responsible for the deaths of over 3 million people. Adolf Hitler was also a progressive turned socialist. Hitler killed at least 5.5 million people he deemed "subhuman". Fidel Castro, a progressive turned communist imprisoned and killed without remorse. The last estimate that I saw said the Castro regime was responsible for over 140 thousand deaths. Pol Pot, another progressive turned communist killed an estimated 2 million people as "enemies of the state". That constituted 25% of his Cambodian countrymen. In short, too much progress too quickly often leads to socialism. Socialism directly caused over 100 million deaths in the past century. Is this the direction our society and government are headed? Is our government embracing the progressive movement to control us like one of these murderous dictators?

The progressive era around the turn of the twentieth century did a lot of good for our country. It brought about more direct democracy, women's suffrage, and antitrust laws. History has shown us that Progress never stops. The progressive era also saw the prohibition of alcohol, which created organized crime in our country. The Ku Klux Klan and eugenics both saw huge rises in popularity during this time. The eugenics movement of the early twentieth century was able to forcibly sterilize over 60,000 "undesirable" American citizens. PBS reports that federally funded sterilization took place in thirty-two states starting in 1907. 64,000 immigrants, people of color, the disabled, unmarried mothers, poor people, and the mentally ill were forced or coerced into being sterilized. A couple of decades later, eugenics was part of the Nazi genocide plan. Was that progress?

Our own republic is a result of progress. It was social progress that inspired the British colonists of North America to revolt against the most powerful empire in the world. Progress allowed those colonists to define the inalienable rights of all people: life, liberty, and the pursuit of happiness. Is the current state of progress what our founding fathers would have envisioned their country to be 240 years later?

All this Progress is expensive. Someone must pay for it. Since the federal government doesn't produce a product to sell, it gets the money from us. Let's take a brief look at that.

Income tax in America was attempted twice prior to the sixteenth amendment. Both times it was judged to be unconstitutional. Then the sixteenth amendment to the constitution was ratified in 1913. In that same year, a 1% tax was levied on income above $3000 and 6% on income above $500,000. It is important to note that $3000 in 1913 would be about $76,000 today and $500,000 equates to about $12.6 million. So, the first legal income tax in this country did not affect anyone making less than $76,000 in today's dollars. Last year the federal income tax rates ranged from 10-37%. Someone making that $76,000 paid 22% ($16,720) for 2018. Add state and local income taxes to the federal and I personally paid almost 27% in income tax last year. Then add 7.45% for Medicare and social security taxes. So, I worked for over four months last year, just to pay taxes, and I don't live in a state with especially high tax rates. Then add state and local sales taxes, property tax, inheritance tax, luxury tax, capital gains tax, gasoline tax, excise tax, and all the other taxes we pay. That is progress from the 0% that I would have paid in 1913 when the income tax was first legally introduced in our country. Is this really the American dream?

As I pointed out earlier, progressivism often leads to socialism. Right now, there are several socialist members of Congress. Elected officials want free college educations, free healthcare, free cell phones, and a litany of other things that they want to give away for free. As I already pointed out, the government does not sell a product or service. They cannot pay for all this free stuff without our tax money. So these progressive politicians want to raise taxes even higher. Let's look at four modern progressive countries for examples of how high. Germany, England, Italy, and Greece all have both income tax and VAT tax (sales tax). The income taxes in these four nations range from 45.8% to 65% and the VAT taxes are between 19% and 24%. So after paying at least 45.8% in income tax you then must pay at least an additional 19% on almost everything that you buy. Combining these two tax types by the country you get total rates from 66.4% to 89%. At what point is it no longer worth working? Why should you or I work at all if Progress will eventually just give us what we need?

Even if the socialist movement goes nowhere, the progressive nature of government is already expensive. Have you ever noticed that anything the government gets heavily involved in gets very expensive? Childcare, college education, vehicles, and healthcare are industries that are all highly regulated. All these industries are increasing in cost far above the rate of inflation. At the same time, the cost of industries not tightly regulated increases at rates below the rate of inflation. Clothing, toys, cell phones, computers, and televisions are examples.

Healthcare presents an interesting opportunity to look at this phenomenon a little more closely. If you include cosmetic surgery and vision care under the umbrella of healthcare, then you have both highly regulated and not so highly regulated segments that can be examined. From 1998 till 2016 the cost of hospitalization and related expenses has increased 177% or roughly three times the rate of inflation. At that same time, the cost of prescription drugs has increased nearly four times the rate of inflation. Those are both stark contrasts to the cost of cosmetic surgery and eye care which have both increased at a rate roughly half of the inflation rate during the same period. When Progress gets involved, costs go up. Then Progress wonders why costs go up and insist on getting even more involved. How much does the government really need to be involved in private business?

Another progressive government trick is what I refer to as tax-payer money laundering. This is done by many organizations. Let's look at Planned Parenthood as an example. According to their own website, Planned Parenthood receives roughly half a billion dollars a year in taxpayer funding. In the 2018 midterm election alone Planned Parenthood donated $30 million to progressive parties and candidates. They may say, "no we don't use the subsidies for that," but money is fungible. If I gave you $100 but specified that you could only spend it on food, that frees up $100 of your own money that you planned to spend on food so you can now spend it however you like. Like it or not, your tax money is helping to pay for the progressive movement. Did you agree to fund the progressive movement?

One of the most effective ways that Progress continues to grow within the government is through temporary programs. Progress sees a problem and then whips up a "temporary" government program to fix the problem. That seems reasonable unless you consider that temporary government programs almost never end. In 1934 the Import-Export bank was created to help fund international business that the private sector felt too risky for investment. In 1945 Congress made the Import-Export Bank permanent. In 1936 the Rural Utility Service was made to help get electricity and telephones to rural America. In 1944 it was made permanent and in 2008 it was expanded to help get broadband internet to rural America. Fannie Mae and Freddie Mac were created in 1938 to buy mortgages from private lenders in order to free up capital during the depression. Now Fannie Mae and Freddie Mac effectively control the entire housing market and were responsible for causing the 2008 housing market crash. In 1935 President Franklin Roosevelt allowed the value of the US Dollar to "float" away from the value of federal gold reserves. In 1971 President Nixon finished this when he announced that the United States was going to be "temporarily" removed from the gold standard. Forty-seven years later US currency still has no connection to any tangible reserves of any value. What is that greenback in your wallet really worth now?

9

Individual Rights

**"Firearms stand next in importance to the constitution
itself."
~George Washington~**

* * *

A growing number of people are lining up to give away their rights. Progress has convinced many people that protecting each others' feelings is more important than the right to free speech. Inclusion has been deemed to be more valuable than your right to worship as you choose. Progress is deciding who does or does not have the right to assemble peacefully. These rights are all defined in the first amendment to the US Constitution. These were judged to be the most important rights that define what it is to be an American. So why has progress recently begun to attack these very rights?

It is our right to speak our minds without fear of reprisal

from the government. Progress wants to limit free speech to only politically correct speech or speech that advances progress itself. That brings to mind another favorite quote of mine. Often wrongly attributed to Voltaire, Hall wrote, "I disapprove of what you say, but I will defend to the death your right to say it." It is the vile and despicable speech that needs to be protected most. It is easy to defend speech that you agree with. Once we allow progress to silence hate speech, how long until progress redefines hate speech?

The second amendment, the right to keep and bear arms, is second in the Bill of Rights expressly to defend the first. Progressives often ask how many guns do you need or why do you need a semi-automatic for hunting? The fact is that the second amendment doesn't have anything to do with hunting. It also doesn't really have anything to do with home or self-defense. What is specifically mentioned in the text of the second amendment is a militia. A militia is an armed citizenry ready for military action. Specifically, military action needed to defend our other rights. Progressives would love to repeal the second amendment. Most won't come right out and say that though. Instead, they use baby steps. They call for restricting the types of firearms we can own, limiting the amount of ammunition we can have, how many bullets a gun can hold, universal background checks, and a firearms registry. Last I checked, criminals don't obey laws, so how do more laws make us any safer? That last one, a gun registry, is historically the last step before mass firearm confiscation. Progress isn't ready for that yet. Progress knows that Gun confiscation in America would cause an immediate and violent revolution. So, progress marches along in increments. When will progress be ready for mass confiscation?

Progressives today may be the first generation in history to lobby for the removal of their own rights. A recent poll of college students showed that 53% believed protecting other people's feelings was more important than your right to free speech. These are the same people who seem to want socialism in America, raising tax rates on the roughly half of us who actually pay taxes. These are the same people who feel so entitled and so special that they demand political correctness at all times in all situations. These are also the same people that want to take away our right to bear arms. Progress is lobbying to take away your right to free speech, take away your right to keep and bear arms and take away your right to keep your own money. What else do they want to take away from the hard-working liberty-loving citizens of our great republic?

Our federal government was designed to have very few specific powers, only thirty enumerated powers are listed for the federal government in our constitution. There are now 430 federal departments, agencies, and sub-agencies according to USA.gov. As government grows, we lose freedoms. Every time some new department, agency, or program is created we lose a little more of our own right to keep our own money. Every time the government wants to give something away, we lose our right to choose. Progress demands that any government continuously grows. As government grows, we lose more control over our own lives, we lose freedoms, and the government just gets more powerful. That is the very reason the powers of the federal government were specifically defined and restricted within our constitution.

Another reason the powers of the federal government were so restricted by our founding fathers was their belief that the best government happens at the level closest to the people. The tenth amendment to the constitution says that any power not specifically listed in the constitution was reserved for the states and the people. In its quest for continuous growth, Progress has found a way around the tenth amendment. Our federal tax dollars are collected, then a portion of that money is offered back to the states with string. Progress says we will give the state millions of your tax dollars for education if you follow the rules of No Child Left Behind, feed the kids according to our rules, test students the way we want, and maintain our standards. Progress will give your state millions of our tax dollars for roads if the state sets speed limits the way progress wants, raises the drinking age to 21, and pass a law requiring seat-belt usage. In short, progress takes our tax money and offers a portion of it back to our state in order to bribe the state government into giving power to the federal government. Is it time to strip our government back to its original powers yet?

10

Revolution?

"Those who make peaceful revolution impossible, make violent revolution inevitable."
~ John F. Kennedy ~

* * *

I firmly believe that the United States is rapidly approaching a second American Revolution. I sincerely hope that it will be a nonviolent revolution that occurs entirely at the ballot box. If the revolution does stay contained within the ballot box, then the citizens will either continue to elect more and more progressive and/or socialist government officials, or those who question the pace or direction of Progress will reject those candidates and elect officials that share their skepticism.

A second option was built in the Constitution of the United States of America. It is called a convention of states. This option is listed in Article V of the Constitution because our founding fathers had the foresight to predict that all government eventually turns tyrannical. The general idea of this process is to call together representatives from all fifty states in a convention. In order to call this convention, thirty-four states must pass resolutions through both houses of their state legislatures. Once thirty-four states have passed the resolution the convention is called for. The convention has only one purpose, to propose amendments to the constitution. These proposed amendments still must be ratified by at least thirty-eight of the state legislatures. The suggested benefit to this solution is that it bypasses Congress. The individual states are in control of this process, not the career Washington politicians. There is currently a movement gaining strength for this second option through an organization called the Convention of States Action. COS Action has fifteen states that have passed the resolution, seven states that have passed it in one chamber, and twelve more with legislative action scheduled for 2019. If all of the states scheduled to look at the resolution this year can pass it, that would be the thirty-four states required to convene the convention. The resolution asks for amendments to be proposed in three areas. COS Action is calling for fiscal restraints to be placed on Washington, term limits on federal officials, and limits to be placed on the power and jurisdiction of the federal government.

A third option would be a violent revolution. No matter who starts violence, the citizens will lose. If the progressive movement takes up arms against the skeptics or if the skeptics are the first to take up arms makes no difference. Thousands if not millions of people will die. I don't want to even discuss this as a legitimate option.

So, let's go back to the ballot box. As mentioned earlier,

throughout history, so many progressive governments have turned to socialism or communism that the mere idea of progressive officials in our government scares me. I understand why so many people like the idea of socialism. Socialism is basically sold to the voters as free stuff. Who doesn't like free stuff? Right now, there is a huge and growing socialist movement in our country, especially among potential voters under thirty years old. I have to admit that when I was in junior high school I thought socialism was a great idea. Fortunately, I eventually realized that there is absolutely no such thing as free stuff. Someone always pays for everything. I also realized that socialism is not a feasible option without eliminating laziness and greed from all people, which is – in a word – impossible. In America, the "someone" who must pay is the fifty-five percent of us who actually pay federal income tax. I know that I have asked this question before, but does this really sound fair?

Socialism as an agent of Progress appears to be quite effective in capitalist nations. I have even read articles that call socialism the next natural step after capitalism. Arguably, America is already quite far down the road to becoming a socialist nation. Here are a few of my questions for those who want Progress to take us the rest of the way down that road. What keeps We The People from becoming even lazier in a socialist society? Just how high will my taxes have to go to pay for all your proposed free stuff? What will keep Americans from starving to death when the money runs out, like what happened in Vietnam, Albania, Argentina, Angola, Yemen, etc.? Why are all the socialist politicians in America filthy rich?

Epilogue

I realize that the majority of people who read this book will either love it or hate it along strict partisan political party lines. I know that most people don't really want to think about these topics at all. Most people just want to listen to their preferred talking head and blindly agree. I also realize that this book will probably be considered controversial, even though I was aiming more for provocative as I wrote it. I am aware that my opinions are obvious to you, the reader, but I have genuinely tried not to tell you what to think. It is my sincere hope that someone might read this book and think about the direction of social progress for a moment. Ask yourself, is the pace of Progress more than society can tolerate? More importantly, is Progress taking us in the right direction? Did Progress start us off on the correct path, but get lost somewhere along the way?

Every step along the path of Progress has unforeseen consequences. One personal example is that I used to stop to try to help every person I saw stranded on the side of the road. Now that almost everyone has a cell phone, I rarely stop to offer help. I just assume they have a phone. With a smartphone, they have access to far more information and help than I can possibly offer. So that is one less act of humanity and compassion on my part. What about the families that we all see when we're dining out in which every member of the family is staring at their phone? In an elevator, waiting in lines, or on public transportation, we used to talk to each other. Now we all stare at our phones. Could anyone have predicted these consequences of an otherwise useful electronic gadget? Having a world of knowledge and entertainment at our fingertips has significantly damaged our desire – and maybe even our ability – to interact socially.

I have attempted to point out how many of the different portions of the modern progressive movement overlap and work together in the march of progress. The insatiable appetite of social progress has many costs. More than just the financial cost of our tax dollars, it is costing us the very rights and freedoms that founded America. The current bloated, over-reaching, progressive federal government has a hand in every segment of social progress. That means we the taxpayers are financing every step of the march. We are financing the elimination of our own rights.

During my lifetime I have witnessed the march of Progress ordered to double time. How long until Progress reaches a full sprint? Where is that sprint going to take our country? Can the world's oldest democratic constitution survive the march?

"Our lives begin to end the day we become silent about things that matter."
~ Martin Luther King, Jr. ~

Afterword

There are several books that I think every liberty-loving American must read. George Orwell's *Nineteen Eighty-Four* is a good start. It illustrates a government with too much control over the people. George Orwell's *Animal Farm* is a short and simple metaphor for every attempt at socialism in history. *Lord of the Flies* by William Golding is another short and simple one. *Lord of the flies* is a story about what happens when popularity becomes more important to a group than the governance. Any book on the fall of the Roman Empire is also a great start. There are many similarities between the last several decades of the Roman Empire and the last few decades of American history.

About the Author

Peter Serefine, Jr. is a proud US Navy veteran, Pennsylvania State Constable, and an average liberty-loving American man and host of Liberty Lighthouse, a talk radio program on Mojo 5-0 Radio. Peter lives with his soulmate, Staisha Hancock, in their big beautiful house in a small Victorian Pennsylvania town.

You can connect with me on:
- https://www.liberty-lighthouse.com
- https://twitter.com/PSerefine
- https://www.facebook.com/PSerefine

Also by Peter Serefine

So Simple A Politician Can Understand
Simple ideas for seemingly complex political issues

Sometimes the answers we seek are so simple that we overlook them. The ideas presented in this book are just that, simple ideas that are largely overlooked. They may not be perfect solutions. They may not even be solutions at all, which is why they are called ideas. The idea for this book struck me during an interview with Cliff Oxford for my show, Liberty Lighthouse. Within a week of that interview, I had begun writing. Over the past two years of hosting Liberty Lighthouse, many simple ideas have come up. This book is a collection of those ideas.

Peter's second book was published on July 4th, 2021.

A More Tyrannical King

"A More Tyrannical King" is a thought-provoking exploration of the shifting dynamics of government power and its implications for the preservation of our cherished principles of freedom, liberty, and limited government. From the perspective of constitutional originalism, this book presents a compelling case that the current federal government has become more oppressive than the despotic rule of King George III during the American Revolution.